Weird and Wonderful Animals

D1732798

NARWHALS

Emma Bassier

DiscoverRoo
An Imprint of Pop!
popbooksonline.com

abdobooks.com

Published by Pop!, a division of ABDO, PO Box 398166, Minneapolis, Minnesota 55439. Copyright © 2020 by POP, LLC. International copyrights reserved in all countries. No part of this book may be reproduced in any form without written permission from the publisher. Pop!™ is a trademark and logo of POP, LLC.

Printed in the United States of America, North Mankato, Minnesota.

102019
012020

THIS BOOK CONTAINS RECYCLED MATERIALS

Cover Photo: John K. B. Ford/Ursus/BluePlanetArchive.com
Interior Photos: John K. B. Ford/Ursus/BluePlanetArchive.com, 1; Todd Mintz/Alamy, 5; Shutterstock Images, 6, 26, 27, 30; iStockphoto, 7, 24; Red Line Editorial, 8–9; Bryan & Cherry Alexander/Science Source, 11; Flip Nicklin/Minden Pictures/Newscom, 12–13, 14, 16 (left), 17 (top), 19, 28, 29, 31; Michelle Valberg/All Canada Photos/Alamy, 15, 17 (bottom); Doug Allan/Nature Picture Library/Alamy, 16 (right); Flip Nicklin/Minden Pictures/SuperStock, 20–21; Pascal Kobeh/

Nature Picture Library/Alamy, 23; David Goldman/AP Images, 25

Editor: Nick Rebman
Series Designer: Jake Slavik

Library of Congress Control Number: 2019942480

Publisher's Cataloging-in-Publication Data

Names: Bassier, Emma, author.

Title: Narwhals / by Emma Bassier

Description: Minneapolis, Minnesota : Pop!, 2020 | Series: Weird and wonderful animals | Includes online resources and index.

Identifiers: ISBN 9781532166082 (lib. bdg.) | ISBN 9781644943380 (pbk.) | ISBN 9781532167409 (ebook)

Subjects: LCSH: Narwhal--Juvenile literature. | Marine mammals--Juvenile literature. | Oddities--Juvenile literature. | Whales--Juvenile literature. | Zoology--Arctic regions--Juvenile literature.

Classification: DDC 599.51--dc23

WELCOME TO DiscoverRoo!

Pop open this book and you'll find QR codes loaded with information, so you can learn even more!

Scan this code* and others like it while you read, or visit the website below to make this book pop!

popbooksonline.com/narwhals

*Scanning QR codes requires a web-enabled smart device with a QR code reader app and a camera.

TABLE OF
CONTENTS

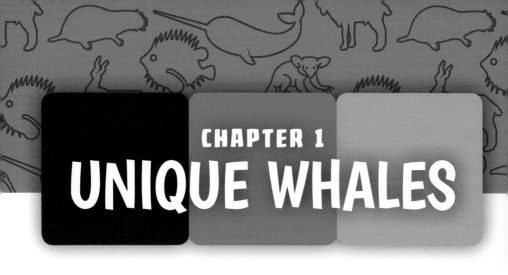

CHAPTER 1
UNIQUE WHALES

Cold, blue water flows past an icy

mountain. Several narwhals swim nearby.

They come to the surface to breathe.

Their pointy tusks stick out of the sea.

WATCH A
VIDEO HERE!

The water temperature in the Arctic Ocean can get as low as 29 degrees Fahrenheit (−1.7°C).

Then the animals go back underwater.

They dive deep to look for food.

Narwhals spend their entire lives in the ocean.

Narwhals are **mammals**. They are a type of whale. Narwhals live in the Arctic Ocean. This ocean is the

northernmost ocean in the world.

Narwhals live in waters near Canada,

Greenland, and Russia.

DID YOU KNOW?

The narwhal's closest relative is the beluga whale.

Similar to narwhals, beluga whales live in the Arctic Ocean.

RANGE MAP

ARCTIC
OCEAN

GREENLAND

CANADA

Narwhal range

N
W E
S

Narwhals live in cold, deep water.

The water is mostly covered by ice.

Narwhals go to the surface to breathe.

They swim through cracks in the ice.

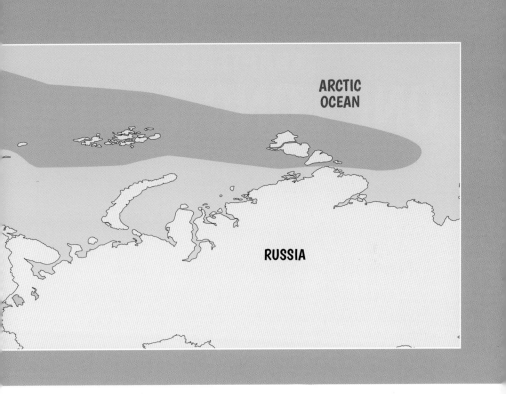

Narwhals **migrate** each year. They move closer to the coast in the summer. That is when female narwhals give birth.

CHAPTER 2
ONE LONG TOOTH

Narwhals are the only type of whale with tusks. However, female narwhals usually don't have them. Males have one long tusk. It grows through the animal's upper lip. The tusk can be up to 8.9 feet (2.7 m) long.

LEARN MORE HERE!

A narwhal's tusk can weigh up to 22 pounds (10 kg).

Female narwhals are approximately
13 feet (4.0 m) long. Males often reach
lengths of 15 feet (4.6 m). A narwhal can
weigh between 1,800 and 3,500 pounds

Narwhals can hold their breath for up to 25 minutes.

(800–1,600 kg). A narwhal has thick skin and **blubber**. Blubber makes up one-third of the animal's body weight.

A narwhal comes to the surface for a breath of air.

Similar to other whales, narwhals

have good vision and large brains.

A narwhal breathes through a blowhole

on top of its head. Its flat tail is called

a fluke. A narwhal also has a flipper on each side of its body.

A narwhal's skin color fades as it ages. Older narwhals are mostly white.

A narwhal shows off its fluke.

LIFE CYCLE OF A NARWHAL

Calves weigh approximately 175 pounds (80 kg) when they are born. They are 5 feet (1.5 m) long. They tend to have gray skin.

Females give birth to babies called calves.

Calves depend on their mother's milk for at least one year. Then they learn to eat other foods and live on their own.

After several years, young narwhals become adults. They can mate.

Narwhals live up to 50 years.

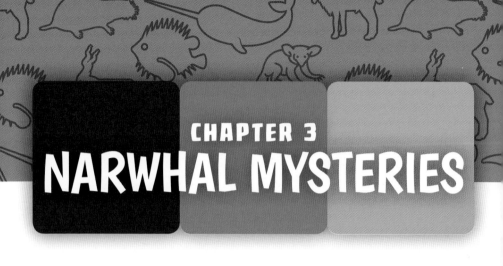

CHAPTER 3
NARWHAL MYSTERIES

Narwhals are difficult to study. Their **habitat** is hard for people to get to. And they often swim away when people get close. As a result, scientists have not seen narwhals mate or eat underwater.

COMPLETE AN ACTIVITY HERE!

A narwhal's tusk has millions of nerve endings that help the animal sense its surroundings.

19

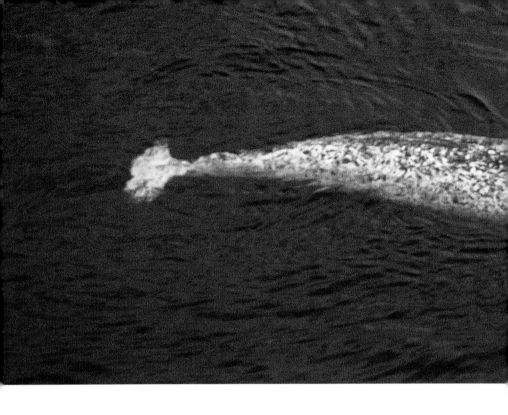

Scientists don't know how narwhals
use their tusks. But they have some
ideas. Narwhals might use their tusks to
sense different chemicals in the water.
Males might also use their tusks to

Some scientists believe narwhals use their tusks to help find food.

attract females. Males may use their long

tusks to show they are old and strong.

DID YOU KNOW?

Narwhals can use their tusks to tell how much salt is in the water.

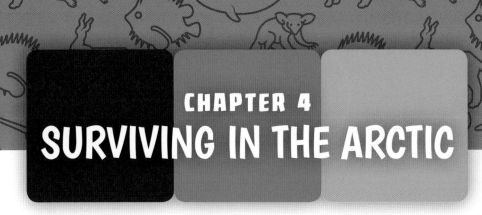

CHAPTER 4
SURVIVING IN THE ARCTIC

Narwhals stay warm thanks to their

thick skin and **blubber**. A narwhal

pumps its fluke up and down to move.

It uses its flippers to change directions.

Narwhals travel in groups called pods.

LEARN MORE HERE!

A pod of narwhals swims through chilly Arctic waters.

Most pods have 15 to 20 members. But

some pods have hundreds of narwhals.

Narwhals sometimes eat cuttlefish, which are related to squid.

Narwhals eat fish, shrimp, and

squid. They suck food into their mouths

and swallow it whole.

Narwhals can dive to

depths of up to 0.9 miles

(1.4 km).

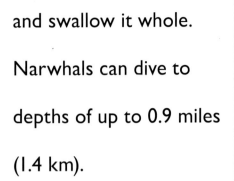

ECHOLOCATION

Narwhals use echolocation to find food and stay away from danger. Echolocation is a method for finding objects using sound waves. Narwhals make sounds that travel underwater. The sounds bounce off objects. Then the sound waves return to the narwhals. These echoes help narwhals locate objects.

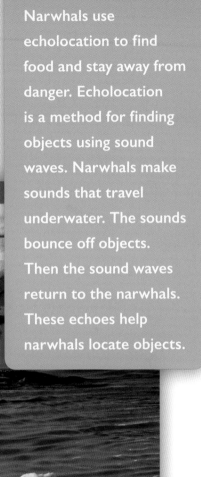

Polar bears sometimes attack young narwhals that are coming up for air.

Narwhals have few predators. But killer whales, sharks, polar bears, and walruses do hunt narwhals.

Climate change is another threat that narwhals face. Climate change causes ice to melt. Predators can easily break thin ice and catch narwhals.

Climate change also causes water

to refreeze more often. When that

happens, narwhals can get trapped. They

can't come up to the surface to breathe.

Walruses may attack narwhals that are trapped in ice.

Native peoples have hunted narwhals for many years.

Narwhals are also threatened by
humans. People hunt narwhals for their
tusks, blubber, and meat. But some laws
protect narwhals. Scientists continue to

study these amazing animals. They want

to help narwhals survive.

DID YOU KNOW?

Narwhals only live in the wild. They cannot survive in **captivity.**

Scientists study narwhals off the coast of Canada.

MAKING CONNECTIONS

TEXT-TO-SELF

Would you like to travel to the Arctic Ocean to see a narwhal? Why or why not?

TEXT-TO-TEXT

Have you read other books about ocean animals? How are those animals similar to or different from narwhals?

TEXT-TO-WORLD

Climate change is causing ice to melt in narwhals' habitats. What other animals could be affected by climate change?

GLOSSARY

blubber – a layer of fat in a mammal that lives in the water.

captivity – when an animal is kept in a zoo or park rather than living in the wild.

climate change – a crisis that is causing Earth's weather patterns to change, often including rising temperatures.

habitat – the area where an animal normally lives.

mammal – a type of animal that has hair or fur and feeds milk to its young.

migrate – to move from one area to another at a certain time.

INDEX

ONLINE RESOURCES

popbooksonline.com

Scan this code* and others
like it while you read, or visit
the website below to make
this book pop!

popbooksonline.com/narwhals

*Scanning QR codes requires a web-enabled smart device with a QR code reader app and a camera.